GRIEF-WISE

Rethinking Grief Support

in the Workplace

Robert Pardi

Grief-Wise, Rethinking Grief Support in the Workplace

by Robert Pardi

ISBN: 9798872664048

First Edition Printed in the United States of America

Dedication

To the courageous souls who navigate the depths of grief, and to those embarking on this journey:

This book stands as a testament to your resilience, a beacon of hope amidst the tempest of loss. Each page is dedicated to the unspoken emotions, the hidden struggles, and the transformative potential that grief holds. May its words echo across boardrooms and office corridors, sparking conversations, empathy, and healing.

To the leaders who dare to redefine corporate landscapes:

May these insights inspire bold change within your sphere of influence. Embrace the power of empathy, nurture cultures of understanding, and lead with compassion. Your commitment to acknowledging and supporting grief in the workplace holds the promise of profound transformation.

To a future where loss no longer means silencing but an opportunity for growth:

Let us reimagine the workplace as a sanctuary for healing, a space where individuals can navigate their grief journey while flourishing professionally. May this book serve as a catalyst for change, propelling us toward a world where every tear is acknowledged, every pain is met with understanding, and every journey through grief is embraced as a path to renewal.

Contents

Rethinking Grief Support in the Workplace

Grief, an inescapable part of the human experience, permeates every aspect of our lives, including our professional endeavors. It is a complex and multifaceted journey that disrupts the very essence of who we are, shaking the foundations of our identity and stability. Yet, within the corporate sphere, grief often remains a silent and invisible force, relegated to the "leave it at the door" box placed neatly to the left of the entrance. This common behavior not only fails to recognize the profound impact of grief on an individual's capacity to function in the workplace, but misses the opportunity to help them recover their shattered sense of self and security.

Loss, in my opinion based on years of working with individuals as well as my own grief journey, is a disruptive tsunami which completely dismantles our sense of self, leaving us adrift in a world suddenly unfamiliar and uncertain. However, within this chaos lies an opportunity—a chance for corporate leadership to proactively address and support grief, instead of it being dismissed or ignored. This will produce a stronger foundation for healing and, honestly, increased employee engagement and loyalty. It is the workplace which is the stability at a time when everything feels adrift.

This e-book posits that the workplace, far from being an escape from grief, can become a catalyst for healing and growth—a space where individuals can reconstruct their identities, rebuild a sense of security, and embark on a journey toward renewal. By acknowledging the nuanced impact of grief, recognizing its transformative potential, and fostering an environment conducive to healing, the workplace can emerge as a beacon of support and rebuilding.

Accept this book as a guide, a loud call for bold change, urging corporate leaders to reassess their approach to grief. It offers a roadmap toward cultivating a workplace culture centered on empathy, understanding, and resilience—a culture that not only supports employees through grief but champions their evolution toward recovery and growth.

Together, let us reimagine corporate leadership's role in acknowledging, understanding, and nurturing the human experience of grief in the workplace. Let us create a world where loss no longer signifies a loss of identity or security, but rather an opportunity for transformation, resilience, and renewal.

How Did I Get Here?

How did I wind up as a grief advocate?

Good question. See, I am an ex-finance executive and was the co-founder of the first boutique private equity firm in Dubai. As my career was reaching heights I only dreamed of, my young wife was diagnosed with late-stage breast cancer, causing me to eventually leave work to help her navigate her illness journey. Unfortunately, she passed eleven years after her original diagnosis.

Returning to the familiar, but seemingly foreign, halls of finance after such a staggering loss, I was met with perplexing advice from colleagues: "Don't talk about the death at work." This directive, while perhaps well-meant, clashed violently with my sense of authenticity. How could I silence the echoes of my deepest pain, masking my humanity behind an emotionless facade? The idea seemed not only wrong but also profoundly dissonant with the depth of humanity itself. Work, the place where we spend a large amount of our lived experience was now a censured existence of superficial tilted head-sighs and pats on the back.

Yet, during this nest chapter, I discovered a longing for change, an undeniable urge to make an impact that resonated far beyond boardrooms and financial portfolios. Fueled by introspection and a desire to rewrite my loss narrative, I embarked on a transformative journey. Leaving my career behind, I charted a course to Italy, embracing a new chapter as a life coach.

My initial foray into coaching immersed me in the realm of grief, a space both raw and tender, yet rich with untapped potential for impact and innovative thinking, yes - I said innovative thinking. Through my work, I witnessed firsthand the transformative power of acknowledging and navigating through grief, not just as an individual experience but as a collective thread that binds us all together.

Guided by this newfound passion, my journey expanded beyond grief into the realms of life transformation, identity shifting, authorship, and speaking engagements. However, grief work has remained a passion as it is a universal human experience, a silent force that urgently demands open dialogue.

I believe it teeters on inhumanity to ask people to leave their grief at the door. It can't be ignored. It is a computer program constantly running in the background which just eats away our available RAM. To live authentically, to step boldly into the future after loss, we must first confront grief openly, acknowledging its presence as a catalyst for transformation.

Join me in what I have learned over the past decade about L.O.S.S. - Lack Of Self and Security

The LOSS Acronym

Lack of Self (Identity Disruption)

Grief can have a devastating impact on an individual's sense of self, particularly when the loss is significant or unforeseen. We often define ourselves in relation to others, and the loss of a loved one can leave us grappling with questions about who we are without that person in our lives. Our identity is also intertwined with our expectations for the future, and the death of a loved one can shatter our plans and dreams. This can leave us feeling lost and adrift, without a clear sense of purpose or direction.

Security

Grief can also erode an individual's sense of stability and safety. The loss of a loved one, especially under sudden or traumatic circumstances, can heighten our awareness of life's fragility and our own vulnerability. This can lead to feelings of anxiety, helplessness, and an amplified perception of threat. We may feel like we are at the mercy of fate, and that our lives are no longer in our own control.

The LOSS acronym underscores the imperative for empathetic support and interventions. These interventions should aim to assist individuals in reconstructing their identity and finding new sources of stability and security throughout their grief journey. Such support holds particular significance in corporate or organizational settings, fostering a more compassionate and accommodating work environment for grieving employees.

Validating the LOSS Concept

Numerous studies have substantiated the correlation between grief and the erosion of identity and security. Research published in the journal **Psychiatry Research** showcased that grieving individuals exhibited notably lower levels of self-esteem and self-efficacy compared to non-grieving counterparts. Similarly, a study in the journal **Death Studies** highlighted increased feelings of helplessness and powerlessness among grieving individuals.

Impact of Losing the "Story"

Central to the LOSS concept is the profound loss of the envisioned "story" for ourselves. The passing of a loved one often shatters the script we had written for our lives, leaving us wandering without a clear direction. This loss of the narrative can be especially devastating for those who defined their future selves by their relationship with the departed, such as spouses, partners, or parents.

Impact of Uncontrollability

The inherent sense of unfairness and uncontrollability surrounding the death of a loved one intensifies the loss of identity and security. This feeling of being at fate's mercy amplifies vulnerability, challenging the stability and predictability of our lives. The sudden and unexpected nature of the loss can further exacerbate this feeling of powerlessness.

I do want to highlight my own journey here. My wife managed metastatic breast cancer for eleven years, and you know what - her death felt unexpected. We are never ready for our loved one's final breath.

Reflect

Acknowledging grief's profound impact on identity and security enables us to empathize more effectively with those experiencing grief, allowing us to provide the necessary support for them to rebuild and discover renewed meaning in their lives.

Navigating Grief in the Workplace: Addressing Cultural Suppression

In the United States, with its strong emphasis on productivity, efficiency, and resilience, the workplace often fosters a cultural norm that discourages open expressions of grief. This suppression of emotions stems from an implicit expectation for individuals to swiftly overcome loss while projecting a composed exterior, despite their inner turmoil.

Cultural Expectations and Workplace Norms

American workplace culture heavily prioritizes professionalism, productivity, and task completion. Implicitly, personal matters, including grief, are expected to remain separate from the professional domain. Employees may feel pressured to conceal or downplay their emotions, striving to maintain an image of competence and fearing being perceived as less capable. Studies within organizational psychology and sociology consistently highlight these workplace norms. Employees often feel compelled to mask their grief due to apprehension of judgment, potential discrimination, or the belief that workplace settings are unsuitable for personal discussions.

Amplifying the Pressure to Suppress Grief

The strong emphasis on productivity and resilience within American culture can exacerbate the pressure to suppress grief. The expectation to "bounce back" quickly after a loss can make it difficult for employees to acknowledge their grief and seek support. Additionally, the expectation to remain professional can make it difficult for employees to discuss their loss with colleagues or supervisors.

The Stigma Surrounding Grief at Work

Grief continues to be stigmatized within many workplaces, especially for men. The fear of being labeled emotionally weak or incapable if one openly expresses grief can deter employees from seeking support or sharing their experiences. This stigma is aggravated by the absence of clear guidelines or policies within organizations on addressing and supporting grieving employees.

Again, there is a wealth of research which underscores the detrimental effects of this stigma. With all of this research, how do we continue to keep the "leave it at the door bucket" to the left of the entrance?

Employees who feel unable to express grief tend to experience heightened stress, diminished job satisfaction, and difficulty focusing on work tasks, ultimately impeding productivity and overall well-being.

The Role of Work in Identity and Stability

While the suppression of grief is widespread in many workplaces, work itself can be pivotal in providing stability and a sense of identity during the grieving process. Work offers structure, routine, and purpose, which can be comforting amid personal upheavals. Engaging in meaningful work positively contributes to self-identity and stability, particularly during periods of grief. Studies affirm that a supportive work environment significantly aids the healing process for grieving employees. When workplaces acknowledge and accommodate grief, offering flexibility, understanding, and support, individuals feel valued, understood, and more inclined to remain engaged and committed to their work.

Strategies for Supporting Grieving Employees

Organizations can implement policies and practices to support employees through their grief journeys:

Create an Open and Understanding Workplace Culture: Foster an environment where employees feel safe discussing their loss, providing empathy and understanding.

Offer Flexibility and Support: Provide flexibility with work schedules and access to resources such as counseling and support groups to aid employees in coping with emotions and navigating grief.

Foster a Culture of Compassion: Encourage compassion and understanding among colleagues to create a supportive environment, reducing the stigma associated with grief.

By acknowledging and supporting grieving employees, workplaces create a more compassionate and supportive atmosphere. Embracing the healing power of work and nurturing a culture of openness and understanding, organizations play a pivotal role in supporting employees through grief, aiding them in rebuilding their sense of self and stability.

Reflect

There is someone you know, at this moment, touched by grief. Someone in your office is dealing with the journey through the valley of the shadow of death.

Navigating grief is a deeply personal and often challenging experience, especially within the workplace. As leaders, recognizing the impact of grief on employees and providing the necessary support during these difficult times is crucial. It's through this acknowledgment and support that workplaces become pillars of strength, aiding individuals in navigating their grief journey while maintaining professional commitments.

By implementing the steps to follow, organizations can create a more supportive and accepting environment for grieving employees, helping them to navigate their loss and maintain their well-being while contributing to the workplace. Here are the seven pillars I have found incredibly impactful which leaders can implement to help support a grief journey by an employee are:

Witness

Include

Safe Space - Buddy System

Reverse Feedback

Future Casting

Respect Boundaries

Celebrate Wins

Witness

Introduction

Grief is nothing to be fixed nor ignored. It is to be witnessed. As leaders, it's our responsibility to create a compassionate and supportive workplace that acknowledges and validates the grief of our employees. By witnessing grief, we demonstrate empathy, let our employees know that their pain is understood, and foster resilience during their difficult time.

Purpose of the Step

Witnessing grief serves as a cornerstone of support, allowing leaders to create a safe environment where employees feel acknowledged, understood, and supported. It's not about fixing their grief, but rather about offering a listening ear, validating their emotions, and providing a sense of belonging. It is about recognizing them as human beings and not as broken objects.

Key Elements

Active Listening: Active listening involves giving your full attention to the person who is speaking, without interrupting or offering unsolicited advice. It's about truly hearing and understanding their feelings and perspectives. When you actively listen, you show that you care about what they have to say and that you value their experience.

Here are some tips for active listening:

Make eye contact and give the person your undivided attention.

Avoid distractions such as your phone or computer.

Nod your head to show that you're listening.

Use verbal cues such as "uh-huh" or "I see" to encourage the person to continue talking.

Paraphrase what the person has said to show that you understand them.

Avoid interrupting or giving unsolicited advice.

Let the person know that you're there for them and that you care.

Active listening is a powerful tool that can help you build strong relationships and support those who are struggling.

Acknowledgment of Loss: A simple yet profound act of empathy and support can make a significant difference for someone navigating grief. While we may never fully comprehend the depth of their pain, conveying our genuine concern and willingness to listen can be immensely comforting. Instead of stating, "I understand your pain," which can be perceived as presumptuous, we can offer more personalized expressions of support such as, "I'm here for you," "I can't imagine what you're going through, but I'm here for you," "I'm here to listen if you want to talk," "Your loss is significant, and I want you to know that I'm here to support you in any way that I can," or "I may not be able to fully understand what you're going through, but I care about you and your well-being." These phrases demonstrate our empathy, respect their unique experience, and reiterate our unwavering support.

Avoidance of Platitudes: Refrain from using clichés like "I know how you feel" or "It's time to move on." These phrases can minimize their experience and make them feel unheard.

Patience and Understanding: Grief is a process, and it takes time to heal. Allow employees to process their emotions at their own pace, avoiding pressure or rushing them through their grieving journey.

Implementation

Open Communication: Create opportunities for open and honest communication, allowing employees to share their grief openly and freely.

Conducting company-wide meetings or workshops to address grief openly and normalize its occurrence in the workplace.

Providing resources and tools to help employees cope with grief, such as access to grief counseling and support groups.

Creating opportunities for employees to connect with each other in smaller, more informal settings, such as grief support groups or peer mentoring programs.

Allowing employees to express their grief in their own way, whether through writing, art, or other creative outlets.

Encouraging employees to take time off work if needed to grieve without fear of repercussions.

By creating an open and supportive environment, you can help employees navigate grief effectively and return to work feeling empowered and resilient.

Flexibility and Accommodations: Provide flexibility in work schedules, workload adjustments, or other accommodations to support employees during their grieving process.

Referring to Support Resources: Provide access to external support resources, such as grief counseling or support groups, to offer additional guidance and coping mechanisms.

Encouragement and Validation: Regularly check in with the employee, express empathy, and offer words of encouragement throughout their grieving process.

Expected Benefits

Reduced Isolation: By acknowledging and validating their grief, employees feel less alone and isolated in their pain.

Enhanced Self-Worth: Validation of their emotions helps employees feel understood and respected, boosting their self-esteem and resilience.

Improved Coping Mechanisms: Witnessing grief provides a safe space for employees to develop healthier coping mechanisms for managing their emotions.

Fostered Trust and Connection: Active listening and empathy build trust and strengthen the relationship between the leader and the employee.

Enhanced Workplace Culture: A culture that embraces and supports employees through grief can create a more compassionate and empathetic workplace environment.

Reflect

Witnessing grief is a powerful way to support grieving employees, fostering a compassionate and empathetic workplace culture. By actively listening, acknowledging their loss, and providing flexibility, leaders can help employees navigate their grief journey while maintaining their professional commitments. This approach not only supports individuals but also strengthens the overall workplace culture, creating a supportive and resilient environment for all employees.

Include

Grief, a profound and complex emotion, can significantly impact an employee's ability to manage their workload and fulfill their work commitments. By actively involving them in shaping their work responsibilities, employers can create a supportive environment that acknowledges their emotional needs and promotes balanced work-life integration.

Purpose of the Step

The primary purpose of inclusion is to empower employees to participate in decisions regarding their work arrangements, giving them a sense of autonomy and control during their grieving process. This collaborative approach fosters a sense of empowerment and reduces feelings of overwhelm, allowing them to focus on their well-being without compromising their professional responsibilities.

Key Elements

Employee Input: Actively seek input from employees regarding their preferences for their workload, deadlines, and work arrangements. This demonstrates respect for their autonomy and allows them to voice their needs and limitations. Examples: Ask them how much they feel would be a positively challenging about of work at this stage.

Collaborative Approach: Work with the employee to create a feasible timeline for their work assignments, considering their emotional well-being and grieving process. This promotes flexibility and ensures that workloads are manageable.

Adaptability: Be open to adjusting work arrangements as needed, acknowledging that grief can fluctuate and affect their ability to work. This flexibility demonstrates empathy and support. Think of a plane that has to course correct – that does not at all negate getting to the final destination.

Implementation

Open Communication: Establish open and honest communication channels, allowing employees to share their needs and concerns openly.

Flexible Work Arrangements: Offer flexible work arrangements, such as remote working flexible hours, or reduced workloads, to accommodate their individual circumstances.

Workload Adjustments: Collaborate with the employee to adjust their workload based on their emotional well-being and ability to cope.

Performance Expectations: Set realistic and achievable performance expectations, considering their grieving process and any adjustments to their workload.

External Support Resources: Refer employees to external support resources, such as grief counseling or support groups, to provide additional guidance and coping mechanisms.

Expected Benefits

Reduced Stress and Anxiety: By actively involving the employee in shaping their work schedule, they experience less stress and anxiety about meeting deadlines and fulfilling their responsibilities.

Enhanced Work-Life Balance: A collaborative approach to work arrangements can help employees strike a better balance between their grieving process and their professional commitments, promoting overall well-being.

Boosted Morale and Motivation: Feeling empowered to participate in decisions regarding their work can boost the employee's morale and motivation, contributing to their overall job satisfaction.

Strengthened Trust and Connection: By involving the employee in decision-making, employers demonstrate trust and respect, fostering a stronger connection and sense of collaboration.

Promoted Workplace Culture: A supportive and inclusive workplace culture that embraces employee well-being can attract and retain talent, creating a positive and compassionate work environment.

Reflect

Fostering inclusion is crucial for supporting grieving employees, promoting a compassionate and empathetic workplace culture. By actively involving employees in shaping their work arrangements, employers can empower them, reduce their stress, and help them strike a healthier balance between their grieving process and their professional commitments. This approach not only supports individuals but also strengthens the overall workplace culture, creating an environment that values employee well-being.

Safe Space – Buddy Up

Introduction

Grief, a deeply personal and isolating experience, can significantly impact an employee's ability to cope with loss and maintain their professional commitments. Creating a safe space within the workplace is crucial for fostering empathy, support, and understanding, allowing grieving employees to navigate their grief while feeling supported and valued.

Purpose of the Step

The primary purpose of establishing a safe space is to cultivate a workplace environment that is compassionate, supportive, and non-judgmental, where grieving employees feel respected, valued, and supported throughout their journey. This step builds upon the foundation laid in Steps 1 and 2, ensuring that grieving employees have a supportive network and resources to assist them.

Key Elements

Open Communication Policy: Encourage open and honest communication between leaders, managers, and employees, allowing them to share their personal struggles without fear of repercussions. This promotes transparency and creates a psychologically safe environment where employees feel comfortable discussing their experiences.

Buddy System: Establish a buddy system. Buddies can offer encouragement, help with tasks, and provide a sense of camaraderie, reducing feelings of isolation and fostering a sense of belonging. The buddy system has the ability to reduce the amount of guilt an employee might feel about not running at their usual pace.

Implementation

Leadership Training: Equip leaders with the knowledge and skills to effectively support grieving employees, including active listening, empathy, and providing appropriate resources. Leaders play a pivotal role in fostering a supportive work culture, and their training is essential for providing the necessary support to grieving employees. This is a great time to bring in guest speakers who have navigated their own grief journeys.

Buddy Matching: Carefully match buddies based on their personalities, communication styles, and availability. Ensure that buddies are sensitive to the grieving employee's unique needs and preferences.

Regular Check-ins: Encourage regular check-ins between buddies and grieving employees. These check-ins can provide an opportunity to offer support, monitor the employee's well-being, and identify any additional needs.

Expected Benefits

Reduced Isolation: By creating a supportive and inclusive workplace, grieving employees feel less alone and isolated in their grief. This sense of community can provide comfort and reassurance, promoting emotional well-being.

Enhanced work-life balance: Flexible work arrangements and open communication channels can help employees strike a better balance between their grieving process and their professional commitments, promoting overall well-being.

Strengthened trust and connection: By fostering a culture of empathy and compassion, leaders can strengthen their relationships with employees, promoting trust and loyalty. This positive work environment can attract and retain talent.

Promoted workplace culture: A supportive and inclusive workplace culture that promotes employee well-being can create a positive and compassionate work environment, attracting and retaining talent. This can contribute to the overall success and reputation of the organization.

Reduced stigma: By normalizing conversations about grief and loss, organizations can help reduce stigma and promote a more empathetic and supportive work environment. This can help employees feel more comfortable seeking support and discussing their experiences.

Reflect

Creating a safe space for grieving employees is crucial for fostering a compassionate and empathetic workplace culture. By establishing open communication channels, providing flexible work arrangements, and implementing a buddy system, organizations can create a supportive environment where grieving employees feel valued, respected, and supported. This approach not only benefits grieving employees but also strengthens the overall work environment, promoting trust, empathy, and a culture of well-being for all.

Reverse Feedback

Introduction

Effective support for grieving employees requires a continuous feedback loop that ensures their needs are met and that the support provided is effective. Reverse feedback facilitates this process by gathering insights from grieving employees about their experiences and identifying areas for improvement.

Purpose of the Step

The primary purpose of reverse feedback is to gather direct feedback from grieving employees about the support they receive from the organization. This feedback provides valuable insights into the effectiveness of existing support mechanisms and helps identify areas where improvements can be made. By soliciting honest and open feedback, organizations can tailor support strategies to individual needs and preferences, fostering a more personalized and supportive work environment.

Key Elements

Regular Check-ins: Leaders schedule regular check-ins with grieving employees to discuss their needs and progress. These check-ins provide an opportunity to address any concerns or challenges the employee may be facing and to ensure that the support provided is meeting their needs.

Inverted Inquiry: Instead of simply asking how the employee is doing, leaders proactively seek feedback on the support provided. This approach shifts the focus from checking up on the employee to genuinely seeking their input on the effectiveness of the support they receive.

Anonymous Feedback: Provide anonymous feedback mechanisms to allow employees to provide honest and open feedback without fear of judgment or repercussions. This fosters a safe environment for employees to share their true experiences and perceptions, ensuring that feedback is unfiltered and unbiased.

Actionable Feedback: Leaders review feedback, identify areas for improvement, and implement necessary adjustments to enhance the support provided. This action-oriented approach ensures that feedback is not just collected but actively used to improve the quality of support offered to grieving employees.

Continuous Improvement: Feedback-driven approach ensures ongoing adaptation and refinement of support mechanisms. By continuously seeking and incorporating feedback, organizations can maintain a dynamic and responsive support system that effectively meets the evolving needs of grieving employees.

Implementation

Establish clear purpose and confidentiality:

Communicate the purpose of the reverse feedback process clearly and consistently to all employees.

Emphasize that feedback will be used to improve support for grieving employees and that their input will be valued and kept confidential.

Provide written documentation of the feedback process, including confidentiality procedures.

Ensure that all leaders and managers are aware of the confidentiality requirements.

Provide anonymous feedback mechanisms:

Offer anonymous feedback forms or surveys that employees can complete confidentially.

Create a dedicated feedback portal on the company intranet or another secure platform.

Ensure that anonymity is maintained throughout the feedback process.

Use a third-party service provider to collect and analyze anonymous feedback, if necessary.

Emphasize non-judgmental attitude:

Model non-judgmental communication in all interactions with grieving employees.

Encourage open and honest communication from employees without fear of judgment or repercussions.

Address feedback in a respectful and sensitive manner.

Avoid making assumptions or generalizations about grieving employees.

Respect boundaries and privacy:

Ensure that feedback is treated sensitively and confidentially.

Avoid sharing feedback publicly or using it to identify individual employees.

Obtain consent from employees before using their feedback in any public or external communications.

Protect personal information and sensitive details shared by employees.

Create opportunities for expression:

Provide multiple opportunities for grieving employees to share their thoughts and feelings openly and honestly.

Offer check-ins, anonymous feedback mechanisms, dedicated support groups, or one-on-one meetings with designated support personnel.

Ensure that opportunities for expression are accessible to all grieving employees, regardless of their location, work schedule, or communication preferences.

Train leaders and managers:

Provide regular training for leaders and managers on how to effectively support grieving employees.

Cover topics such as active listening, empathy, non-judgmental communication, and the importance of confidentiality.

Role-play feedback sessions and provide feedback on leadership performance.

Encourage leaders and managers to seek guidance from human resources or other support professionals when needed.

Ensure accessibility:

Make sure that feedback mechanisms are available to all grieving employees, regardless of their work location, schedule, or communication preferences.

Offer options for feedback through in-person check-ins, online surveys, phone calls, or other accessible channels.

Provide translation services for employees who speak different languages.

Proactively address concerns:

Promptly address any concerns or feedback raised by grieving employees.

Show genuine concern and empathy for their experiences.

Take action to address the concerns raised, keeping employees informed of progress.

Thank employees for their feedback and demonstrate that their input is valued.

Maintain open communication:

Keep grieving employees informed of progress on their feedback suggestions.

Provide regular updates on the implementation of feedback-driven changes.

Encourage open communication and feedback from employees throughout the process.

Foster a culture of transparency and accountability.

Incorporate feedback into support strategies:

Actively incorporate feedback into the development and refinement of support strategies.

Use feedback to identify areas for improvement and make data-driven decisions.

Monitor the impact of feedback-driven changes and make adjustments as needed.

Maintain a continuous cycle of feedback and improvement.

Benefits

Enhanced Support: Feedback helps leaders tailor support strategies to individual needs and preferences. By gathering specific insights from grieving employees, organizations can personalize their support offerings, ensuring that each employee receives the support that best suits their unique situation.

Improved Communication: Open and honest feedback fosters open communication and trust between leaders and employees. This transparent approach creates a psychologically safe environment where employees feel comfortable seeking support and discussing their needs openly.

Empathetic Workplace Culture: Feedback-driven approach cultivates an empathetic and supportive work environment. By actively seeking and addressing the needs of grieving employees, organizations demonstrate their commitment to compassion and create a culture of care and support.

Continuous Improvement: Feedback-driven approach ensures ongoing adaptation and refinement of support mechanisms. By continuously collecting feedback, organizations can identify areas for improvement and adapt their support strategies to remain relevant and effective over time.

Reflect

By implementing reverse feedback, organizations can create a more compassionate and supportive workplace environment for grieving employees, fostering their well-being and contributing to their overall success within the organization.

Future Casting: Forward Momentum and Motivation

Introduction

Grief can significantly impact an employee's outlook on the future, making it challenging to reconnect with their passions, aspirations, and goals. Future casting, a proactive approach to support grieving employees, aims to rekindle hope and motivation by engaging them in conversations that focus on their future aspirations, dreams, and goals.

Purpose of the Step

The primary purpose of future casting is to provide grieving employees with a platform to explore their interests, identify potential career paths, envision a positive future, and rediscover their sense of purpose, direction, and motivation. These conversations foster resilience and optimism, enabling employees to navigate their grief with greater clarity and determination.

Key Elements

Future-Oriented Conversations: Establishing a regular cadence of check-ins to discuss the employee's future aspirations, dreams, and goals. These frequent conversations provide a safe space for employees to explore their interests, identify potential career paths, and envision a positive future. Learning something new could be valuable to moving forward through grief. This would be a time to investigate potential new trainings for the employee based on future goals.

Safe and Supportive Environment: Creating a non-judgmental and compassionate atmosphere where the employee feels comfortable sharing their thoughts, feelings, and aspirations. This supportive environment fosters trust and encourages open communication, allowing employees to express their emotions freely and openly explore their hopes and dreams.

Active Listening and Empathy: Demonstrating active listening by paying close attention to the employee's perspectives, validating their emotions, and offering understanding and support. Active listening shows genuine concern and helps employees feel heard, validated, and respected.

Achievement-Focused Goal Setting: Collaborating with the employee to set realistic and achievable goals for the next twelve months, breaking down larger goals into smaller, manageable steps. Goal setting provides a sense of direction and helps employees stay motivated as they work towards their objectives.

Celebration and Encouragement: Acknowledging and celebrating milestones achieved towards these goals, reinforcing a positive outlook and providing encouragement throughout the journey. Recognizing progress reinforces the employee's belief in their abilities, motivates them to continue pursuing their goals, and fosters a sense of accomplishment and self-efficacy.

Implementation

Regular Check-ins: Scheduling regular one-on-one meetings with the employee to discuss their future goals and aspirations. The frequency can vary depending on the employee's needs, but weekly or bi-weekly check-ins can be beneficial. Consistent check-ins help maintain a focus on the future and ensure regular progress.

Empathetic Approach: Creating a safe and supportive environment where the employee feels comfortable sharing their thoughts, feelings, and aspirations. Actively listen to their experiences and empathize with their challenges. Active listening and empathy build trust and encourage the employee to open up about their experiences.

Goal Setting Collaboration: Working with the employee to set realistic and achievable goals that align with their interests, passions, and career aspirations. Encourage them to break down larger goals into smaller, more manageable steps. Collaborative goal setting ensures that the goals are relevant, achievable, and tailored to the employee's individual needs and aspirations, promoting a sense of ownership and motivation.

Milestone Celebrations: Regularly recognizing and celebrating the employee's progress towards their goals, reinforcing their sense of achievement and motivation. This could include public recognition, small rewards, or a simple "thank you" for their efforts. Celebrating milestones keeps the employee engaged, motivated, and recognizes their accomplishments, boosting their confidence and fostering a sense of progress.

Resource Provision: Offering support and guidance in identifying and accessing resources within the organization that can help the employee achieve their goals. This could include mentorship opportunities, skill development programs, or access to relevant projects. Providing resources empowers the employee to take action towards their goals, increases their chances of success, and demonstrates the organization's commitment to their well-being.

Benefits

Renewed Purpose: By engaging in future-oriented discussions, leaders help grieving employees reconnect with their passions, rediscover their sense of purpose, and envision a positive path forward. Future casting helps employees identify their strengths, interests, and aspirations, guiding them towards a fulfilling future.

Motivational Boost: Engaging in goal setting and celebrating achievements can provide a much-needed boost of motivation and encouragement, helping employees navigate their grief while maintaining their professional commitments. Setting goals

35

provides a sense of direction and purpose, while celebrating milestones reinforces their belief in their abilities.

Resilience and Hope: By fostering a focus on the future, leaders can help grieving employees build resilience and foster a hopeful outlook for the future. Future casting helps employees identify their potential, envision a positive future, and develop a growth mindset, promoting resilience.

Personal Growth: Future casting encourages employees to explore new interests, expand their skill sets, and identify opportunities for personal growth. This can lead to new career paths, increased job satisfaction, and a sense of personal fulfillment.

Enhanced Engagement and Productivity: By reconnecting with their aspirations and setting achievable goals, grieving employees are more likely to feel motivated and engaged in their work. This can lead to improved productivity, reduced absenteeism, and increased organizational success.

Stronger Workplace Culture: A culture that supports employee well-being and encourages future-oriented thinking can foster a sense of belonging, empathy, and shared purpose among employees. This can lead to a more positive and productive work environment for all.

Reflect

Future casting is a valuable tool for supporting grieving employees as they navigate their grief and rediscover their goals and aspirations. By engaging in future-oriented conversations, setting achievable goals, and celebrating milestones, leaders can help grieving employees regain a sense of hope and motivation, enabling them to move forward with purpose and confidence. This approach not only benefits grieving employees but also strengthens the overall workplace culture, promoting resilience, empathy, and a focus on the future.

Respect Boundaries

Grief can profoundly impact an individual's emotional state, making it challenging to engage fully in their work responsibilities. During this sensitive time, it's essential for leaders to respect and uphold the grieving employee's boundaries regarding communication, workload, and social interactions.

Purpose of the Step

The primary purpose of respecting boundaries is to create a safe and supportive environment where grieving employees feel comfortable and empowered to navigate their grief without feeling overwhelmed or pressured. By respecting their preferences and limitations, leaders can foster a sense of understanding and empathy, enabling employees to focus on their well-being without compromising their work commitments.

Key Elements

Respect in Communication:

Initiation: Allow the employee to initiate conversations about their grief. Avoid prying or repeatedly bringing up the topic, giving them control over the pace and depth of their disclosure.

Frequency: Respect their preferences for communication frequency, whether it's daily check-ins, weekly updates, or more sporadic interactions. Adjust communication based on their emotional capacity and needs.

Mode: Adapt to their communication preferences, whether it's face-to-face meetings, virtual chats, or email exchanges. Ensure communication channels are comfortable and accessible for them.

Respect in Workload:

Flexibility: Be flexible with their workload and deadlines, allowing for adjustments based on their emotional capacity and needs. Consider offering temporary reductions or adjustments as needed.

Supportive Workload: Distribute tasks in a way that minimizes their stress and prioritizes their well-being. Collaborate with them to identify tasks that can be delegated or adjusted.

Open Communication: Discuss any concerns regarding their workload and work performance with empathy and understanding. Work together to find solutions that are mutually beneficial.

Respect in Social Interactions:

Sensitivity: Be mindful of social interactions, avoiding forced participation in social gatherings or unnecessary group activities. Respect their desire for privacy and avoid pushing them to socialize prematurely.

Patience: Allow them to gradually re-engage in social interactions at their own pace. Recognizing their need for time and space to process their emotions is crucial for their well-being.

Understanding: Acknowledge that grieving employees may need more time and space to process their emotions and adjust to social settings. Be patient and understanding of their needs.

Implementation

Open Dialogue: Initiate a conversation with the employee to discuss their preferences regarding communication, workload, and social interactions. This open dialogue fosters transparency and mutual understanding.

Empathetic Approach: Listen attentively to their needs and concerns, demonstrating empathy and understanding. Show that you care about their well-being and are willing to support them during this difficult time.

Adaptive Strategies: Implement strategies that respect their boundaries and support their well-being, such as adjusting communication frequency, workload, or social engagements. Collaborate with them to find solutions that work for both parties.

Regular Check-ins: Schedule regular check-ins to assess their needs and make adjustments as needed. This regular communication demonstrates your ongoing concern and support.

Respect for Privacy: Respect their privacy and avoid sharing personal information about their grief with others. This confidentiality will help them feel comfortable and respected.

Expected Benefits

Reduced Stress and Anxiety: By respecting their boundaries, employees feel less pressure and anxiety, allowing them to focus on their grief and mental health without feeling overwhelmed by work demands.

Enhanced Work Performance: A supportive and respectful environment can lead to improved work performance as employees experience greater emotional stability and well-being.

Strengthened Organization Culture: Respecting boundaries fosters a compassionate and understanding company culture that values employee well-being and fosters trust among colleagues.

Mitigated Turnover Rates: By creating a supportive and respectful work environment, organizations can reduce the risk of employee turnover, especially among those facing personal challenges like grief.

Reflect

Respecting boundaries is an essential step in supporting grieving employees. By creating a safe and supportive environment where they feel comfortable and empowered to navigate their grief without feeling overwhelmed or pressured, organizations can foster a compassionate and understanding company culture that values employee well-being and fosters trust among colleagues. This approach not only benefits grieving employees but also strengthens the overall workplace culture, leading to reduced stress and anxiety, enhanced work performance, and mitigated turnover rates.

Celebrate Achievements

Introduction

Grief can significantly impact an individual's emotional well-being and their ability to perform at work. During this challenging time, it's crucial to recognize and celebrate their achievements, both big and small, to uplift their spirits, maintain their motivation, and nurture their resilience.

Purpose of the Step

The primary purpose of celebrating achievements is to acknowledge and appreciate the grieving employee's contributions, both significant and incremental, reinforcing their value within the organization, maintaining their motivation, and fostering resilience in the face of their challenges.

Key Elements

Active Recognition: Regularly acknowledge their contributions to the team, highlighting their accomplishments through verbal praise, written feedback, or public recognition. This active recognition demonstrates appreciation and reinforces their value.

Focus on Small Wins: Celebrate both large and small achievements, no matter how insignificant they may seem. Recognizing even minor progress reinforces their efforts and helps them maintain momentum.

Personalized Recognition: Tailor your recognition to the employee's preferences and interests. Understanding their unique motivations allows for more personalized and meaningful recognition.

Variety of Recognition Methods: Use a variety of recognition methods to keep the experience fresh and engaging. This could include verbal praise, written feedback, public recognition, or even small rewards or tokens of appreciation.

Consistency and Timeliness: Maintain consistency in your recognition to ensure they feel valued and appreciated. Recognize their achievements promptly to maximize their impact and boost their morale.

Meaningful Connection: Connect their achievements to their personal goals and aspirations. This enhances their sense of accomplishment and reinforces the relevance of their work.

Implementation

Regular Check-ins: Schedule regular check-ins with the grieving employee to discuss their work performance and accomplishments. This ongoing dialogue provides opportunities to recognize their efforts and offer praise.

Highlight Achievements: At the end of each project, meeting, or task, take a moment to recognize the employee's contributions. This could involve verbal praise, written feedback, or small gifts or tokens of appreciation.

Public Recognition: Publicly acknowledge the employee's achievements during team meetings, company newsletters, or social media posts. This wider recognition can boost their morale and reinforce their value within the organization.

Meaningful Rewards: Offer rewards or incentives that align with the employee's interests. This could involve tickets to a sporting event, gift certificates to their favorite stores, or donations to charities they support.

Celebrate Milestones: Recognize significant milestones in their grieving process or career development. This could include completing a training program, achieving a performance goal, or successfully managing a challenging situation.

Expected Benefits

Uplifted Spirits: By acknowledging and appreciating their accomplishments, leaders can demonstrate their support and uplift the grieving employee's spirits, helping them navigate their grief with a sense of encouragement.

Maintained Motivation: Celebrating their progress, regardless of size, can help maintain their motivation and drive them to continue contributing despite their grief. Recognition reinforces their belief in their abilities and encourages them to persevere.

Fostered Resilience: Recognizing their achievements fosters resilience and encourages them to persevere through their challenges. Positive reinforcement and acknowledgement of their capabilities can help them develop a growth mindset and overcome obstacles.

Strengthened Employee Engagement: Celebrating achievements demonstrates that the organization values their contributions and cares about their well-being. This can enhance employee engagement, leading to increased productivity and job satisfaction.

Promoted a Culture of Recognition: By consistently recognizing and appreciating employees, organizations can cultivate a culture of appreciation and support, fostering a sense of belonging and community. This positive workplace culture can positively impact employee morale and retention rates.

Reflect

Celebrating achievements is an essential step in supporting grieving employees. By recognizing and appreciating their contributions, both big and small, organizations can help maintain their motivation, foster resilience, and uplift their spirits during this challenging time. This positive reinforcement can also strengthen employee engagement and create a culture of appreciation and support within the organization.

Guiding Grieving Employees Through the Workplace: A Seven Faceted Approach for Leaders

Witness

Recognize and acknowledge the grieving employee's loss by expressing heartfelt condolences, lending a listening ear, and demonstrating empathy. This simple act of validation provides invaluable comfort and support during these challenging times.

Include

Foster a sense of connection and belonging by facilitating opportunities for the grieving employee to stay involved with colleagues and the workplace. Encourage their participation in team meetings, social events, or informal gatherings, which can alleviate feelings of isolation and support their emotional well-being.

Safe Space - Buddy System

Establish a safe and supportive environment where the grieving employee feels comfortable expressing their emotions and seeking assistance. Consider implementing a buddy system, pairing the employee with a compassionate colleague who can be a second pair of hands, offer guidance, encouragement, and a listening ear.

Reverse Feedback

Collaborate with colleagues to gain insights into the grieving employee's workload, communication preferences, and overall well-being. By soliciting feedback, we can identify areas where additional support and accommodations are needed to ensure their success.

Future Casting

Encourage conversations about the grieving employee's future goals and aspirations. This process helps them reconnect with their passions, career aspirations, and find hope and direction amidst grief, fostering a sense of purpose and resilience.

Respect Boundaries

Adhere to the grieving employee's personal boundaries regarding communication, workload, and social interactions. Avoid intrusive inquiries or pressuring them to return to their usual routine prematurely; instead, allow them to progress at their own pace while ensuring their well-being is prioritized.

Celebrate Wins

Acknowledge and celebrate the grieving employee's achievements, both big and small. This positive reinforcement uplifts their spirits, maintains motivation, and nurtures resilience. Encourage access to external support resources, such as counseling or grief support groups, to provide additional guidance and coping mechanisms.

Reflect

By implementing these seven steps, leaders can effectively support grieving employees, empowering them to navigate their grief while maintaining professional commitments.

By creating a compassionate and supportive work environment, we can foster resilience, enhance well-being, and ultimately, strengthen our organizations.

Call to Action for Leaders

Grief is a universal human experience that can profoundly impact an individual's ability to work effectively. As leaders, we have a responsibility to create supportive and compassionate work environments that foster the well-being of our employees, especially those navigating the difficult journey of grief.

By implementing the seven steps outlined in this guide, you can empower your grieving employees to navigate their grief while maintaining their engagement and contributing to the organization's success. Remember, every employee matters, and their well-being is inextricably linked to the overall health and productivity of your team.

Closing Thoughts: A Call to Transform Workplace Culture

As this journey through the intricacies of grief in the workplace comes to a close, we stand at a pivotal crossroads. The insights shared within these pages aim not merely to inform but to incite change – a change that begins with each leader who holds the power to shape workplace dynamics.

Embracing a New Vision: Leadership isn't merely about steering teams towards goals; it's about fostering a culture where humanity thrives. Our workplaces are more than just hubs of productivity; they are sanctuaries for growth, healing, and collective empowerment.

The Imperative of Empathy: To lead in a world of complexities, leaders must don the armor of empathy. Recognizing the multifaceted nature of grief isn't a weakness but a strength, an acknowledgment of our shared human experience.

A Call to Action: It falls upon each leader to rewrite the narrative surrounding grief. Let us no longer avert our eyes but meet grief head-on, offering understanding, support, and a nurturing environment for those traversing this challenging path.

Transformative Leadership: To build resilient, thriving workplaces, we must champion a transformative leadership ethos—one that upholds empathy, values emotional well-being, and prioritizes the holistic growth of every individual within our organizations.

Embracing Regenerative Corporate Cultures: Beyond acknowledging and supporting individuals through grief, let us embrace the concept of regenerative corporate cultures. These cultures strive not only to mend wounds but to cultivate environments where growth, healing, and evolution are woven into the fabric of daily operations.

The Time for Change is Now: Now is the time for action. Let us weave a tapestry of understanding, compassion, and support within the fabric of our workplaces. Together, we can create environments where grief is acknowledged, respected, and met with the unwavering support it deserves.

Join the Movement: I invite you to join this movement toward transformative leadership. Embrace empathy, lead with compassion, and foster workplaces that not only acknowledge grief but serve as beacons of support and growth for every individual within them.

Your Role as a Leader: Your role as a leader extends beyond tasks and targets; it's about sculpting a culture where every individual feels seen, heard, and valued. Embrace this transformative potential and be the catalyst for change within your sphere of influence.

Reflect

As we move forward, let us shoulder the mantle of empathy and resilience. Let our workplaces be the foundation upon which the edifice of compassionate leadership is constructed—an enduring testament to our unwavering commitment to embracing the human experience in its entirety.

Thank you for embarking on this journey. Now, let us forge the future of work, one compassionate step at a time.

About Robert

Amidst life's most profound transitions, Robert Pardi emerges as a beacon of transformative leadership, his life a testament to the power of personal transformation. His unwavering belief in the limitless possibilities that life holds, coupled with his unwavering commitment to action, has empowered countless individuals to overcome challenges and achieve their dreams.

Robert's journey began in the world of finance, where he excelled as a senior portfolio manager for the Abu Dhabi Investment Authority. His expertise and leadership skills brought him into contact with top leaders from around the globe, providing him with a global perspective on the world of business and leadership.

However, life took an unexpected turn when his young wife was diagnosed with late-stage breast cancer. This devastating news forced him to confront the fragility of life and the strength of the human spirit. As he and his wife embarked on their arduous journey, Robert drew upon his inner resilience and unwavering belief in possibilities, co-founding the first boutique private equity firm in Dubai.

Despite his remarkable achievements, Robert's greatest challenge lay ahead. As his wife's condition worsened, he took a sabbatical to be by her side, supporting her to achieve her dreams as she approached the end of her life. In the wake of her passing, Robert found solace in his desire to share the life lessons he had learned, transforming his grief into a catalyst for personal growth and transformation.

He embarked on a new chapter, relocating to Italy and immersing himself in the world of life coaching and motivational speaking. His passion for self-discovery and leadership development led him to author several books focused on intentional living, grief, and transformation.

Robert's impact extends beyond traditional boundaries, as he reshapes the landscape of grief, personal growth, and leadership development. His profound insights and unwavering belief in human potential have left an indelible mark on those he guides.

You can learn more about his work at: http://www.robertpardi.com

www.ingramcontent.com/pod-product-compliance
Lightning Source LLC
Chambersburg PA
CBHW062254290526
45794CB00006B/2549

* 9 7 9 8 8 7 2 6 6 4 0 4 8 *